How Gamification Can Help Your Business Engage in Sustainability

Paula Owen

paula@paulaowenconsulting.co

www. paulaowenconsulting.co.uk

www.ecoactiongames.org.uk

T0303979

Published by Greenleaf Publishing Limited

Aizlewood's Mill

Nursery Street

Sheffield S3 8G

UK

www.greenleaf-publishing.com

Printed and bound by Printondemand-worldwide.com, UK

ISBN 978-1-909293-40-3 (eBook-ePub)
ISBN 978-1-909293-41-0 (eBook-PDF)
ISBN 978-1-909293-39-7 (Paperback)

A catalogue record for this title is available from the British Library.

Page design and typesetting by Alison Rayner
Cover by Becky Chilcott

DōShorts

Dō Sustainability is the publisher of **DōShorts**: short, high-value ebooks that distil sustainability best practice and business insights for busy, results-driven professionals. Each DōShort can be read in 90 minutes.

New and forthcoming DōShorts – stay up to date

We publish 3 to 5 new DōShorts each month. The best way to keep up to date? Sign up to our short, monthly newsletter. Go to **www.dosustainability.com/newsletter to sign up to the Dō Newsletter.** Some of our latest and forthcoming titles include:

- *Green Jujitsu: The Smart Way to Embed Sustainability into Your Organisation*   Gareth Kane
- *How to Make your Company a Recognised Sustainability Champion*   Brendan May
- *Making the Most of Standards: The Sustainability Professional's Guide*   Adrian Henriques
- *Promoting Sustainable Behaviour: A Practical Guide to What Works*   Adam Corner
- *How to Account for Sustainability: A Business Guide to Measuring and Managing*   Laura Musikanski
- *Sustainability in the Public Sector: An Essential Briefing for Stakeholders*   Sonja Powell
- *Sustainability Reporting for SMEs: Competitive Advantage Through Transparency*   Elaine Cohen
- *Sustainable Transport Fuels Business Briefing*   David Thorpe
- *The Changing Profile of Corporate Climate Change Risk* Mark Trexler & Laura Kosloff

- *The First 100 Days: How to Plan, Prioritise & Build a Sustainable Organisation*   Anne Augustine
- *The Short Guide to Sustainable Investing*   Cary Krosinsky
- *REDD+ and Business Sustainability: A Guide to Reversing Deforestation for Forward Thinking Companies*   Brian McFarland
- *Adapting to Climate Change: 2.0 Enterprise Risk Management* Mark Trexler & Laura Kosloff

Subscriptions

In addition to individual sales of our ebooks, we now offer subscriptions. Access 60+ ebooks for the price of 6 with a personal subscription to our full e-library. Institutional subscriptions are also available for your staff or students. Visit **www.dosustainability.com/books/subscriptions** or email **veruschka@dosustainability.com**

Write for us, or suggest a DōShort

Please visit **www.dosustainability.com** for our full publishing programme. If you don't find what you need, write for us! Or suggest a DōShort on our website. We look forward to hearing from you.

....

Abstract

A NEW, INNOVATIVE ENGAGEMENT theory has been quietly permeating the business world over recent years, and it answers to the name of 'gamification'. In a relatively short time, the ideas and thinking behind gamification have begun to circulate through the corporate community and beyond, and are now causing widening ripples of interest in other more diverse sectors of society. The term, virtually unknown just a few years ago, is now being widely discussed, and its concepts implemented, in sectors as diverse as health and fitness,[1] medical research,[2] the financial sector[3] and through to even achieving the seemingly impossible task of making mundane domestic chores[4] exciting. Its relatively early accomplishments in these areas throw up an intriguing question for sustainability professionals: 'If it works successfully in these sectors, what might be its potential for encouraging pro-environmental engagement and behaviour change in the environmental sector?' The main goals of gamification are increased user interaction, behavioural change and the stimulation of innovative thinking and the generation of new ideas. But what is gamification in practice? Is it simply the latest 'flash-in-the-pan' techie-led fad? Does it actually have the substance required to establish itself as a genuinely useful business tool for deepening and strengthening engagement? Moreover, and more importantly for organisations concerned with enhancing their environmental sustainability, can it be developed and implemented in such a way as to help persuade customers, employees, shareholders, executives and board members

ABSTRACT

alike to become more sustainable in their purchasing habits, everyday working lives and investment choices? This DōShort investigates and reports on the current state of play (no pun intended), thinking and theories concerning gamification, and its potential role in deepening the level of engagement in the sustainability agenda, in this its early stage of evolution. It draws together the emerging facts, examples of early adopters and existing practice to help businesses decide whether the tools of gamification can be applied in engaging their own customers, staff and other stakeholders in more sustainable practices.

....

About the Author

PAULA OWEN has worked in sustainability for over two decades. She began her career in academia, gaining a PhD in climate change chemistry from Oxford University. However, she quickly realised she couldn't spend her entire life in darkened laboratories and so changed tack slightly to concentrate on the communicating of environmental and scientific concepts and issues to general audiences.

Since then she has worked for environmental charities, within in the public sector, through secondments in central government, and in 2010 she set up her own research, authorship, training and advice agency focusing on environmental sustainability generally, and energy and carbon management in particular. She relishes the challenges of working with a diverse selection of clients from blue chip companies, environmental charities, through arts and funding bodies to international NGOs.

She is a published author and has written widely on the subject of energy efficiency within the domestic sector. She was the project manager for the award-winning UK Government's Act on CO_2 carbon calculator.

Over the past years she has become more convinced that behaviour change and engaging the majority is vital if we are to make progress environmentally. In 2012 she was awarded a London Leaders position by the London Sustainable Development Commission, and Unltd Social Entrepreneur award funding, to further her work in researching the power of fun and games to help save the planet.

Acknowledgments

I WOULD LIKE TO THANK Nicoletta Landi for her help as both a researcher on the case studies used in this book and for her skill at proof-reading and language checking and Jamie Beevor for passing his reliably analytical eye over my more fanciful ideas and flowery prose and keeping me in check.

Contents

An innovative, novel engagement theory has permeated the business world over recent years. In a relatively short time the ideas behind 'gamification' have begun to circulate through the corporate community and beyond, and are now causing widening ripples of interest in diverse sectors of society. This DōShort investigates the thinking around gamification in this early stage of its evolution and asks the question: how may it play a part in advancing the sustainability engagement agenda?

This section discusses what gamification is. It is currently touted by global players and thought-leaders as the new business tech trend to watch, and is already being tested out in a diverse range of sectors, but what does the term actually mean and what do its theories entail in practice? Crucially, could it have relevance to the sustainability sector?

In this chapter we play with the building block concepts of gamification. We identify and explain the individual tools in this new compendium set and illustrate their use in environmentally focused examples. This chapter also identifies the various pieces of the jigsaw needed to 'gamify' a process of your own.

Gamification could have much potential to help sustainability professionals get the environmental message across to staff, executives, customers and stakeholders in a positive, inspiring and engaging way. Not only useful as a communication and engagement tool, it is also being advocated as a potent behaviour change agent.

Here we look at a number of examples of eco-gamification in action across the business sector and across the world, which have already been tried and tested and are bearing results.

The case to prove whether gamification will be a useful long-term engagement tool for sustainability is still in its infancy. To date it has shown early promise and delivered some impressive results in other sectors, medical research and health and fitness applications being stand out examples. Its use as a sustainability engagement tool has also delivered some initial early success stories in areas of transport, employee engagement, energy and recycling as described in this book. In this section we explore the potential for future gamification in sustainability and make suggestions for how a business could develop its own sustainability 'game plan'.

CHAPTER 1

Introducing Gamification: A Flash in the Pan or the Next Big Thing?

A short history of gamification

IN 2005, A US-BASED START-UP company began exploring the potential of using the established theories of social games and games mechanics, taking and translating the concepts and applying them to non-game situations and sectors. This novel approach was seen to work successfully in a variety of contexts over the following years and, consequently, a new business engagement concept was born. That company was called Bunchball[5] and its founder, Rajat Paharia, coined the term 'gamification' for the first time around the year 2010 to give the concept an identity.

In just a few years, the broad concept, theories and practices of gamification have taken off in a diverse range of sectors. The business world has begun to embrace the idea to help it find new and compelling ways to engage with its customers, its staff and other stakeholders. Gamification advocates claim it offers the potential for businesses to gain competitive advantage, deepen relationships with customers and retain their custom for longer. From the employee engagement perspective it is claimed to help improve productivity, increase staff morale and lead to an increasingly engaged, more hard-working and switched-on workforce.

INTRODUCING GAMIFICATION:
A FLASH IN THE PAN OR THE NEXT BIG THING?

By utilising similar principles that make both traditional games and online social media games appealing and compelling, i.e. encapsulating a sense of fun, competition, achievement, gratification, improvement and rewards, businesses are beginning to take notice of its potential. In particular, they are looking to gamification to increase that holy triumvirate of staff productivity, customer loyalty and, of course, bottom-line profitability. Crucially, it also provides an alternative way in to reach out to a younger sector of consumers, customers, clients and potential employees: basically the strata of society born around and after 1990, brought up in a wholly digital age and nicknamed 'Generation Y' or the 'digital natives', those who have never known a pre-Internet world. This sector of society is often somewhat impervious to the traditional methods of communication and advertising and requires something much more interactive, novel and challenging to engage their attention in any meaningful and long-lasting way.

Finding a single dictionary definition of gamification that is universally adopted is difficult. The gamification wiki,[6] probably the largest compendium of information on the subject, offers the following definition:

> Gamification is the concept of applying game-design thinking to non-game applications to make them more fun and engaging. Gamification can potentially be applied to any industry and almost anything to create fun and engaging experiences, converting *users* into *players*.

The idea of turning 'users', a relatively reactive term, into 'players', a term that suggests proactive engagement, effort and activity, is a key element of the gamification process. The notion of evolving passive consumers or employees from simply recipients of products/services or commands/

orders respectively into active, engaged, enthusiastic proponents of whatever the organisation is 'selling' is a powerful driver for businesses. To convert both customers and staff into positive and vocal advocates for the brand has a strong pull and, indeed, marketers have been using this approach for some time. This is why, in these early days of the evolution of gamification, businesses are beginning to prick up their ears and take note of the early successes in this area.

Indeed, a Gartner report[7] released in 2011, predicted that by 2015 more than 50% of organisations that are involved in innovation processes would be 'gamifying' those processes, and, it reported, in a matter of just a few years the ideas of gamification, for consumer marketing and customer retention, would be just as important as those behemoths of twenty-first century engagement and commerce: Facebook, eBay and Amazon. The main goals of gamification, according to Gartner, are increased user interaction, behavioural change, the stimulation of innovative thinking and the generation of new ideas. Wouldn't that be a breath of fresh air in the increasingly rather stale world of employee engagement initiatives and other environmental improvement programmes?

Deloitte, in their Tech Trends report,[8] devote a whole chapter to the topic, and have come up with their own snappy definition: 'gamification is about taking the essence of games – fun, play, passion – and applying it to real-world, non-game situations'. They cite it as one of their Top Ten trends to watch over the coming years and highlighting 2012 as the year that 'gamification moves beyond entertainment to business performance, using intuitive design, intrinsic motivation and the sense of accomplishment that comes from completing activities with clear and personal values'.

Deloitte goes on to say: 'In a business setting, that means designing solutions using gaming principles in everything from back-office tasks to training to sales management and career counselling.'

The very idea of games, online gaming and 'gamers' being at the heart of the development of any seriously debated, potentially important business tool might seem anathema to some. Anyone who feels that computer or other 'online' games, particularly of the 'shoot 'em up' variety, are just a colossal waste of time may have a particularly hard time swallowing the potential of gamification as an effective business engagement technique. However, what is becoming increasingly apparent is, by exploring the pared-down principles of good games design and applying the fundamentals of game mechanics to existing processes, there appears to be a tremendous amount of potential for the business community.

The gender-based argument that any type of 'gaming' focused solution, business related or otherwise, would only appeal to males, and to a certain more youthful age bracket, also seems to not hold water as the average game player today clocks in at a mature 37 years old and over 40% of all game players are female (McGonigal, 2011).

Indeed, already we have seen successful gamified applications in widely diversified areas: for example, in health and fitness,[9] where there is a whole host of online applications, such as myfitnesspal and Fitocracy, that help individuals lose weight and take up more exercise through the use of online score (calories consumed versus calories burnt) keeping, sharing successes with friends in an online community and daily challenges. In medical research[10] we see the phenomenal success of the Foldit project which is discussed in Chapter 2; and on to the financial sector[11] where the online help tool Saveup.com, for example, allows people to more easily manage their money through making financial management into a game. Finally, there is even the 'sexing up' of mundane domestic chores[12] a hitherto seemingly impossible challenge overcome by a simple online game, Chore Wars, which turns completing household tasks into a challenge within household or office environments of who can score the most points, top the leader board and win prizes by completing otherwise shunned and oft-avoided tasks.

The influential US-based Pew Research Center, as part of their 'Pew Internet and American Life project', recently published a report into the future of gamification[13] as predicted by a survey of over one thousand internet experts, tech analysts, critics and stakeholders. In it they concluded that experts 'generally believe the use of game mechanics, feedback loops and rewards will become more embedded in daily life by 2020'.

They went on to predict that the results of such a 'gamification' process could have both positive and negative consequences. On the plus side, they said that the 'move to implement more game elements in networked communications will be mostly positive, aiding education, health, business and training'. However, they also signed a note of caution regarding the potential for 'invisible, insidious behaviour manipulation' through the use of such interventions.

Indeed, already we are seeing reports of the nascent gamification industry being worth $100 million, and that is predicted grow to $2.8 billion by 2016 according to a 2012 forecast[14] by M2 Research, a US-based analysis firm, that is assessing the trends in gamification worldwide.

So what does the idea and implementation of 'gamification' principles within a sustainable business environment entail? Moreover, how can these principles be applied to environmental improvement and engagement in sustainability generally? We discuss these questions next.

What role for gamification in educating for sustainability?

This DōShort argues that gamification has much potential as a new method for engaging people – staff, stakeholders, consumers, customers and clients – in environmental action. But how is it different to what has gone before? Moreover, can it offer new insights into the complex area of motivation, retention and action for sustainability in the longer term? To frame these questions we look back at the world of environmental campaigning and educating over recent decades.

Ever since the emergence of an organised global environmental pressure movement in the early 1970s, through the creation of pressure groups such as Greenpeace, a predominant focus of campaigns to galvanise the public into action has been on the doom and gloom, 'act now or pay later' style of campaigning. For many acute situations and environmental disasters, such as oil spills or deforestation, company malpractices or single issue debates, such as Greenpeace's early focus on 'saving the whale', inciting a sense of injustice, anger and possibly even guilt (i.e. implying that inaction could signify a passive acceptance of the situation) worked effectively in mobilising hundreds of thousands of latent activists across the globe to take action – whether directly or through a more 'armchair activism' approach of monetary donations to the cause.

The 1970s and 1980s, in particular, saw the rise of the amateur environmentalist – ordinary citizens with a passion for the issues and a strong understanding of the original cause of the problem and the ultimate effect that it was having, and how they could help to solve the situation by clear, unambiguous actions. Reasonably clear-cut, 'cause and effect' issues were the typical campaign route. They were typically localised (but not always), and generally had a clearly defined 'enemy' to be thwarted – be it the CFCs in aerosols that were destroying the ozone layer, or the pollution from dirty factories that caused 'acid rain' resulting in lakes and rivers hundreds of miles away becoming poisoned and lifeless. People could take action, whether it be boycotting aerosol cans, tuna from unsustainable companies or products from factories that were causing the pollution; they felt empowered and crucially believed that their actions could and would make a positive difference. The feedback loop also, although not by any means instantaneous, did report that slowly, but steadily, such concerted, individual actions were truly making a difference – the ozone hole was slowly repairing itself, poisoned lakes were coming back to life and fishing companies were changing their unsustainable practices.

Roll on to the early years of the twenty-first century and those clearly identified, reasonably unambiguous environmental nemeses of the past have been more or less superseded by a more obscure, disparate, multi-faceted foe. Issues that used to be neatly defined, pigeon-holed and dealt with through focused, results-driven campaigns now manifest themselves as much more complex, equivocal and harder to pinpoint the cause and effect. They are typically argued about endlessly on the TV, in print media and on the new democratising medium of the World Wide Web.

We are talking, of course, about the environmental issue that has trumped all others in terms of its global significance and long-term potential for disruption – accelerated, anthropogenic climate change. It is with this globally weighty, but messy and indistinct issue that the environmental sector's players – those being the activists, campaigners and communicators – missed a trick when it came to the vital task of informing, educating, inspiring and galvanising the wider public into taking positive, pro-environmental action against climatic change. Despite being a new issue, the methods employed to communicate it remained firmly anchored in the past. Potentially a reflection of an 'if it ain't broke, don't fix it' mentality, the issue under discussion may have changed, but the tone and approach of delivering the message has remained the same. The 'scare them with the bare facts and they are bound to take action' approach worked in the past, so who was to say it wouldn't work this time around?

Consequently, the approach to climate change communications and education has tended to focus on the 'doom and gloom' aspects – which, of course, are understandable: there is a lot to be gloomy about! However, the sheer vastness of the issue, combined with the non-acute, longer-term, probability-based range of potential effects, and continuing debates on the uncertainties of the science, did and do little to inspire ordinary folk into action. Indeed, the opposite effect can occur, with people arguing themselves into inaction as they do not believe that they alone, as individuals, can actually make any impact whatsoever in solving this issue.[15]

Typically, calls to action on climate change related issues have tended to lean towards the 'misery messaging' end of the communication spectrum, with a large dollop of guilt thrown in for good measure. The 'change your ways or the polar bear will die' style of campaigning may work on small children and the 'charismatic mega fauna' enthusiasts amongst us, but is not a message that will inspire sustained, practical action in the masses.

A backward glance at the rather unfortunate film media advertising campaigns of both the UK government's 'Act on CO_2' (a primetime TV advert where a father is reading a bedtime story to his child about how climate change would soon devastate their environment and most famously featuring a drowning puppy[16]) and the campaign group 10:10's ill-conceived, Richard Curtis-penned short film *No Pressure*[17] where children and adults who didn't take carbon-reducing actions were graphically blown up in a range of locations, are a few extreme examples on how badly in the wrong direction the climate change messaging and 'calls to action' have veered over recent years.

In the grand scheme of things, a bad news story, or a guilt-tinged messaging campaign will have some short-term success. It will have an effect on latent, would-be greenies who need that last nudge into taking action. For people who have guilt as a motivator in their lives this approach can also work. However, it is not an approach that alone will enjoy mass appeal and engage the majority to take action in the longer term.

This is where gamification can step into the breach. As, by its very nature, it is a positive, inclusive, action-oriented approach to education, influencing and ultimately behaviour change, it could be a major 'game changer' in the sustainability world. The appeal of games, in their broadest form and manifestations, are their very wide multi-generational draw. Most people, at some point in their lives, have played and been absorbed by a game – from simple single-player cards games such as Patience and Solitaire to that kids' perennial favourite Trumps, to chess,

Scrabble, Monopoly, Cluedo and Risk, all the way through to the earliest electronic games such as Tetris, Space Invaders and bringing it up to date with the hugely popular Massive Multiplayer Online (MMOPS) type of game such as World of Warfare.

Games are fun, and unless you are a particularly sore loser, one's experience of playing them is typically rewarding, entertaining, occasionally educational (Trivial Pursuit, Scrabble or trump style games, for example) and generally sociable. Hence the idea of using some of the underlying concepts that make up the theory and practice of games design and mechanics to bring a fresh approach to education and engagement in environmental issues seems, in theory at least, a reasonable starting point for a method of engagement.

Before moving on to discuss the implications of gamification on environmental issues, it must be made clear that this is not advocating the trivialising of an issue as globally disruptive and serious as climate change by attempting to turn it into a game. Instead we are exploring the potential of turning communications, educational initiatives and 'calls to action' pertaining to climate change and other environmental issues, into more positive messages around how such actions can be aspirational and constructive to assist widespread take-up.

To explore some of these ideas we first need to look at the concepts that gamification is based on, namely: the ideas of social games and social media games, game mechanics and game design techniques. We look more closely at these concepts in the next chapter.

....

CHAPTER 2

Elements of the Theory: The Lego Set of Gamification

ALTHOUGH HAILED AS AN INNOVATIVE, twenty-first-century business tool, gamification has its roots firmly planted in the science and art of game mechanics and design that go back decades if not millennia. The modern idea of using games and gaming techniques as a model for re-defining and re-imagining existing processes is borne from the research and writings of leading online games developers and thought-leaders such as Jane McGonigal, Gabe Zicherman and Jon Radoff (see further reading for references). Interestingly, all three of them have brought out best-selling books exploring various aspects of gamifying real life, business and marketing in the last few years.

McGonigal, in her seminal book *Reality is Broken: Why Games Make Us Better and How They Can Change the World*, provides a strong argument around the power of games as a tool to re-engage people in societal change. In it she argues that modern life, as millions of us live it in the developed world at least, often ceases to provide the interesting, rewarding, absorbing, satisfying hard work that most of us crave – consciously or subconsciously. This is why, she posits, online games, computer-generated worlds and gaming generally have become so tremendously popular in recent decades.

This other virtual, alternative world, where ordinary folk can become heroes, take on seemingly impossible challenges and lead teams to victory over digital foes, are supplying people with the hit of satisfying hard work they need, giving them a purpose and a challenge and making them feel worthwhile, if only for a few hours a day. She quotes (rather large) figures for the typical number of hours US gamers spend online playing these types of game – 13 hours per week, by an estimated 183 million people. There are, according to McGonigal, 100 million regular gamers in Europe, 200 million in China and 105 million in India. People would much rather quest after imaginary trophies and dazzling jewels, fight tirelessly to slay virtual enemies, free captive team mates or dignitaries and continually attempt to 'level up' to the next set of challenges, seemingly not put off by repeated failures and the number of real-life hours lost to the virtual challenge.

What if, she suggests, we could use the elements and proven devices of games theory and design, not to simply create imaginary worlds where millions, if not billions of people, can lose themselves for hours at a time, but to create real-life social change? Imagine how powerful that could be? Harnessing the collective brain power and ingenuity of these eager 'warriors' and putting their combined effort to good, real, practical, positive use. It's an extremely powerful thought.

Indeed, this thought has already been put to the test through the phenomenally successful computer based *Foldit* experiment devised by medical researchers at the University of Washington. In 2011, would-be amateur science researchers around the world were challenged to attempt to decipher the protein structure of a monkey virus known to cause AIDS. Understanding and replicating this molecule was of critical importance to researchers in their fight to cure the disease. It attracted over 46,000 'players' who took part in the 'gameplay' over an originally timetabled, fixed period of three weeks. Participants received points for taking part and were awarded higher points the more complete and accurate their developed protein structure became. Remarkably, within just 10 days of the challenge, contributors had come up with an incredibly accurate model of the key enzyme that had kept professional medical researchers baffled for well over a decade.[18] This discovery has significantly advanced progress in the fight to defeat AIDS and it was achieved in less than a fortnight by a motley group of tens of thousands of unpaid, amateur enthusiasts – an impressive feat.

So, persuaded that this is an approach worth investigating further, how and where do you start to get your head around what a gamified approach to sustainability could look like?

What follows is a discussion of the various gamification 'Lego' bricks. We explore the building blocks of how it can be constructed, with the aim of giving you a simple 'starter guide' to the tricks and techniques behind bringing gamification into your business.

We start with a few basic definitions of common terms used in gamification theory such as social games, games mechanics and game design:

Social games

Social games are, at their simplest, games that are played with other people. Hence games such as Solitaire, Patience and Sudoku would not tend to fall into this category. Social games typically have the following characteristics:

- They have well-defined rules that must be followed

- They are for two or more players

- There is a pre-determined outcome or set of outcomes that signify the end of or stages in the game

- There is usually a winner (or at least an attainment of a certain level of the game by an individual or team)

- Each player has to expend effort of some type in playing the game

- Each player has a stake in the outcome of the game

Social games have a long history, with the earliest recorded dice games being found in Asia dating back to prehistory, and the first board game being found in a burial site in Egypt dating to circa 3500 BC. Another very early example of a social board game, the Royal Game of Ur, discovered by an explorer in the deserts of Iraq in the 1920s, seemingly a game played by Sumerian royalty and buried with them, can even be played online today at a British Museum website that has recreated it for a twenty-first-century gaming audience.[19]

Modern manifestations of social games are known as *social network games*, in other words, games that are typically played online through a social networking site. Social network games are some of the most popular games played in the world today with tens of millions of players, and some of their most famous incarnations are Happy Farm, Farm Ville and The Sims Social. Then there are the rather impressively titled 'Massively Multiplayer Online' (MMO) games, such as World of Warcraft which claims to be the biggest paying game community in the world with over 11.5 million registered players in 2010 (McGonigal, 2011).

One of the defining aspects of these multi-player games is that they engender a sense of 'community' even if this community is almost entirely virtual. The games tend to be shared by players through their online social networks, via Facebook, Bebo and the like. Hence the more popular games tend to quickly go 'viral' with little need for expensive, widespread marketing and PR campaigns.

The predominant route for 'gamification' solutions to date has been online and most recently the medium has developed further through the use of mobile apps. Some of the most popular games, however, are not necessarily completely novel nor indeed modern – for example, one very popular mobile app download is that most traditional of board games, Scrabble, which has been transformed for the twenty-first century by the idea of the scrabble board and letter counters being held in 'cloud', hence a game can be played between yourself and a cousin in Australia, for example, over an asynchronous time period that suits both parties.

Game mechanics

Game mechanics at their simplest are the 'rules and tools of engagement'. A defining element of what constituents a game is that it must have a number of rules, contrived boundaries or 'terms of engagement' by which would-be players voluntarily sign up to be constrained whilst playing. These can be simple, straightforward guidelines on the 'Dos and Don'ts' of the game, through to very complex, multi-layered instructions that reveal themselves as the game progresses or as you attain new levels. The various mechanics of the game can interact with each other to develop the level of complexity, and dictate the level of engagement of the players themselves.

Game design

The elements of game design are the true building blocks of a game, and they come together to form the gameplay and the mechanics/rules and give any particular game its unique character and feel. A number of the most common components of game design, and the elements most often seen in gamification techniques, are discussed below.

One size doesn't fit all

When planning a gamified process it is useful to think about categorising your potential audience into player types, a simple classification of the different general types of games players. This was originally derived by a UK-based games designer, Richard Bartle, who was a pioneer in the early development of multi-user dungeons, or MUDs. In reality, not as sinister as they may sound but simply the evolution of traditional games into online-based alternative virtual worlds that could be entered by many people to play with others from the comfort of their own desktops – the original online social media game format. From studying the users of MUDs, Bartle started to classify players into four main types:

- Achievers

- Explorers

- Socialisers

- Killers

Achievers: as the title suggest, this type of player wants to win. They want to master the game, they want to unlock the next level. They are interested in mastering new skills and hitting those targets and then moving on to the next challenge. This can be as an individual or within a team. Their main motivations are to overcome, get better, achieve and conquer the challenge.

Explorers: these are the curious. They enjoy the unlocking of new pathways, discovering hitherto unknown ways of playing and progressing; they like to understand the terrain and discover new techniques.

Socialisers: socialisers want to be liked. They are more interested in the team playing, sociable aspects of games and gaining the respect of their peer group. They will respond to more cause-based challenges. They often like to lead but to gain that position through popular vote.

Killers: for killers it's all about the competition. They really, really want to win. They want to beat the competition and see themselves topping the prize board. For killers all's fair in love, war and games.

Naturally, all games cannot appeal in equal measure to each of these broad categories, and an early consideration of your typical potential audience is useful in deciding what type of game mechanics you want to develop. However, if you can devise a gamified approach that appeals to at least two of these categories of player, you are widening the appeal of the challenge and encouraging broader participation.

How to 'gamify' a process

We have defined the various aspects of game development from which gamification derives. We now turn to the components of game design and describe some of the most common techniques used to 'gamify' processes. Sustainability-focused case studies are used to help to bring the elements to life and describe a real-life initiative where they have been utilised and results seen.

Fundamentally, a process is thought of as being 'gamified' if it exhibits at least one, but usually several, of the following features of game design:

Leader boards

Leader boards, or some other visual way of displaying the 'state of play' and the relative positions of the players/teams is useful for keeping people's interest and momentum up. If these boards can display in 'real time', or near to it, information on the relative progress of participants, so much the better as this has an instantly gratifying effect of keeping people involved, engaged and participating, whether it is to maintain their pole position, or to 'up their game' and push through the rankings. Human nature dictates that people like to see themselves as compared to others, hence where there is a competitive element and the chance of topping a 'league' in such a visual, public way, continued participation is enhanced.

Attainment levels ('levelling up')

Levelling up is an important concept in games mechanics and design, and is used frequently to reward sustained effort and ensure players do not lose interest as soon as they have conquered one level of the game. A well designed gamification intervention should have a number of levels or attainment stages to ensure enthusiasm and interest is maintained over time.

The term 'levelling up' has been adopted in the gaming world to describe the notion of working hard and persistently to beat the obstacles and challenges at a current level. In this sense, 'winning' is defined as completing that particular set of challenges or attaining a particular skill set, with the reward typically being the 'unlocking' of the next level of the game. The player then, in essence, heads straight back to a 'square one' position on the next, higher, typically more challenging level. The whole effort to 'level up' then starts again with renewed enthusiasm as new challenges present themselves.

Most of us can relate to the experience of being gripped by a desire to 'beat' a game, whether it be Tetris, Space Invaders, Angry Birds or a multitude of other ultimately pointless, but totally addictive, lone player games, only to lose interest completely the moment you 'conquer' that particular game. Without higher levels to master that replace the conquered task, then interest quickly wanes and it is typically not picked up again. Hence the importance of ensuring any challenge or competition is 'multi-levelled' in some respect in order to sustain enthusiasm and engagement over the longer term, but to also ensure that the increase in difficulty level is gradual so as not to turn players off by a sudden leap.

Rewards for effort expended

A key constituent of many successful online social media games and interactive membership-style sites is the idea of gaining 'rewards' in exchange for effort expended. These rewards do not necessarily have to be of a real cash value or indeed be real in any meaningful way. They do however need to be visible, and they require a 'value' in the eyes of the 'community' that needs to be easily communicated and recognised by others. This is illustrated by the plethora of online retail and other community-based sites where one earns 'rewards' in the shape of badges, stars, tokens, special privileges, etc. for engaging in some form of effort, assistance to others or focused activity. Online communities and shopping sites give rewards for user reviews of products purchased, events attended or experiences undertaken. Contribute enough of them, and you become a star member, your opinions valued more than the masses and hailed as a guru on the topic. For example, with Amazon, the reward for your reviewing efforts is to become a star reviewer and be featured on their site as such. Few of these rewards amount to much more than having a virtual gold star next to your username, but it is the kudos of achieving the status that drives members to expend much voluntary effort writing reviews or otherwise contributing time and energy to the cause.

Recognition badges

Following on from the idea of 'rewards', the achieving of certain levels, tasks, etc., are often recognised with an achievement badge. An old and well-established form of this is the idea of achieving activity badges in groups such as the Scouts and the Brownies, for example. Children proudly display their 'recognition of success' on the arms of their uniforms; the desire to attain these badges and, more importantly, display them to your peer group, is a powerful motivational tool.

Feedback loops

One of the key elements of a gamified process is the idea of constant and constructive feedback on effort undertaken and progress made. A manifestation of a feedback mechanism is the idea of a 'leader board' as described earlier, but feedback can and should go much further than that. Feedback on performance, given immediately after effort has been expended, for example in a points rating or qualitative ranking on this attempt as judged against an earlier effort, means that the individual can learn and act on the information in an immediate and positive way. Feedback, even when it is reporting back an ultimately failed endeavour, if given objectively and constructively, can encourage the player simply to try harder next time, getting back on that horse immediately after taking a tumble. A feedback mechanism that can capture any positive improvements, for example, a slightly faster time to completion, a higher total percentage rating or a generally more complete solution to the challenge, is also useful reinforcing the idea that each time a person tackles a task, they get better in some way, shape or form. This is a powerful motivational technique.

Eco case study: Fiat 500 eco driving[20] software

A good illustration on how feedback loops have been implemented successfully in the transport sector is the addition of eco-driving software and visualisation tools of performance in the dashboards of cars. The Fiat 500 has introduced a simple downloadable software solution called **eco:Drive**. The software is downloaded onto a computer and a USB stick is plugged into the dashboard; as the car is driven, information about the journey is captured. That data can be then uploaded onto a computer and the driver's style and performance analysed. The driver is given a score out of 100, the 'eco Index', for his/her effort on that occasion and given tips on how to improve next time (levelling up). There is a dashboard to monitor fuel and carbon saved, and to monitor personal performance and improvement over time. In addition, there is a function to set yourself challenges to improve your 'eco Index' by a self-selected value. There is also an online community of eco:Drive users – this community displays a cumulative score of total CO_2

saved by the entire community of Fiat ecoville members that, at the time of writing, weighed in at an impressive 4500 tonnes of CO_2 and has nearly 70,000 members. Fiat claims that drivers can save up to 15% on their fuel bills by using the app.

Credits

Similarly to rewards, the expending of effort and the achievement of certain tasks, or milestones can lead to the earning of credits and/or points. These can be real, i.e. to be spent on goods or services; or virtual, in terms of buying more privileges within a game. A number of successful environmentally focused initiatives rely on the idea of people earning 'credits' for good work done, for example in recycling their rubbish, that they can then go on to spend in the high street. Crucially, this type of credit is not awarded for simply buying more stuff at a particular supermarket, or only buying fuel from a certain chain of petrol stations – that type of approach is simply a straightforward loyalty or incentive scheme. Instead, these gamified processes require action, effort and/ or behavioural change to be rewarded with credit. Recyclebank is a well-established example of this type of gamification technique.

Eco case study: Recyclebank

Recyclebank originated in the United States and is now available in the UK. They claim to have four million members worldwide. It is a credit-based initiative that rewards people who join the scheme and register their recycling and other pro-environmental efforts with credits that can then be spent in participating retailers and other service providers on the high street. The more they participate, and the more friends they recruit, the more points they receive. Alternatively, people can donate their credits to a number of approved schools projects, where Recyclebank turns the points into a cash donation to the school.

Peer-to-peer comparison

The need to compare oneself with one's neighbour, work colleague, family member or another in one's social circle is innate – the idea of 'keeping up with the Jones's' hasn't remained a well-worn cliché for so long without good reason! In the absence of any other metrics by which to measure social standing or level of expertise in a subject or activity – the comparison with someone you recognise as your equal more generally is an important benchmark.

This type of technique must be used with caution however, as if the comparison is too broad or general or deemed irrelevant – for example, a national average, sector average or if perceived not to reflect the individual's own view of themselves – there is a risk they will not engage or switch off from the process entirely. A useful illustration of how this gamification technique has been deployed in the environmental sector, with varying degrees of success, is discussed next.

Eco case study: Act on CO_2 Carbon Calculator Comparator Tool

An early output of the UK government's general climate change education and communication campaign, Act on CO_2 was an online, interactive, engagement tool – the Act on CO_2 Carbon Calculator.[21] This footprinting calculator was developed for the domestic sector and its original aims were: to increase carbon literacy throughout the British public; allow citizens to calculate their own household and/or individual carbon footprint arising from their use of energy/transport fuels; and to provide users with a personalised action plan to assist in engagement with energy efficient activities to reduce their carbon footprint. It provided an instant feedback mechanism in that as soon as the user had input energy and fuel usage data, they received their carbon footprint value. Users were then encouraged to do a peer-to-peer comparison through comparing their measured footprint to a 'National Average' footprint value, derived through taking the total emissions for the domestic sector and dividing that by the number of households in the UK. The calculator proved to be popular and received over a million visits in the first year with a completion rate of around 40%.

However, research into the user experience of interacting with the calculator and the potential for it being a behavioural change tool brought interesting unforeseen consequences to light. Users, after completing their footprint, were encouraged to explore the results section of the website to help them put their footprint value into context. They then explored the 'call to action' features, which consisted of a dynamically generated, personalised action plan, predicated on their answers, with the intention of encouraging them to take up the suggested pro-environmental actions. The functionality that allowed comparison of an individual's footprint result with that of the national average uncovered two curiously challenging issues. The first insight was that a number of users, who saw their footprints were higher than the national average carbon footprint, became dismissive and defensive when confronted with this unfavourable comparison. They maintained they could not be compared to the national average, as they and their lifestyles/family situations were not 'average' and hence the comparator was not valid; in other words they were not prepared to accept the tool as a true peer-to-peer comparator and so dismissed the result. Instead, they maintained, if they could only be compared to 'people like themselves' – with similar homes, family size, lifestyle, etc., then that would be a more accurate and subsequently relevant comparison tool.

The second issue to emerge was that some users who came in lower than the national average could express a tendency to be complacent with their current score. Hence they felt they could disengage with the notion of further action to reduce their carbon footprint as they were already doing 'better than the average' and so felt they had 'done their bit' for the environment.

This posed a dilemma for the project team, as it was important that the calculator, as well as being an educational tool and a visually engaging way of explaining a carbon footprint, was also a tool for further engagement and pro-environmental behavioural change.

The addition of the peer comparison with a nationally derived average value, was in some cases (but not by any means all), disappointingly proving a disincentive to further action.

However, after over two years of use, the tool had collected approximately one million sets of carbon footprints from a wide range of household sizes and types, and this raised the possibility of developing a 'people like me' style comparator tool,[22] based on the totally anonymised dataset, which could potentially overcome the issue of users who initially disregarded the national average comparison. This functionality was developed and released in a second edition. Early user testing research revealed that this type of highly personalised peer-to-peer comparator functionality resonated more strongly with users. It also removed a particular barrier to action in the subset of users who disengaged primarily because they did not feel the national average comparator was appropriate or useful for them.

The learning from this case study is that a peer-to-peer comparator can be a very powerful tool in gamification processes, but the comparison metrics must be felt to be appropriate by its intended audience, otherwise it may have the unintended, contrary effect of disengaging the exact audience it was meant to engage.

Public pledges

Pledges, resolutions or promises, whether made in a public way or not, have been a mainstay of environmental and health-related campaigns for many years, with, to be frank, mixed levels of success. An important key to ensuring that any promise or pledge is adhered to is to ensure they are made in a way that is available to significant others, whether family, friends, community group or work/teammates, to view and informally 'police' through peer pressure.

Publicly made declarations of intent, or pledges, especially if made to assist or help others, have the most likely chances of success. The impression that you would be letting others down if you break your pledge, as opposed to simply letting yourself down, is a much more powerful motivator, and suggests that it could act as a powerful driver to keep someone on the straight and narrow, more than individual willpower alone.

Eco case study: The DoNation

A novel form of 'pledging' for pro-environmental actions can be seen in the innovative, cashless sponsorship website platform The DoNation.[23] The DoNation takes the well-established idea of sponsoring friends and family to perform various heroic deeds of athleticism such as running a marathon or completing a triathlon, but instead of the person asking for money, they ask their friends, families and colleagues to sponsor them in simple sustainability actions with the metric of saved carbon emissions as the quantifiable 'score'. The number and types of actions, or 'DoActions' as they are called on the site, that have been pledged are added to the sponsored person's public 'totaliser' page on the website and the accumulated amount of carbon saved by all the pledgees is calculated and displayed.

This is a very public and permanent display of the pledgees and their pledges made. In addition, typically, as the group of people sponsoring an individual are usually part of either a tightly or loosely knit peer group – as at the very least, they all have the sponsored person in common, the obligation to actually carry out your pledged action is felt more strongly by the individual – they don't want to be the one that is seen to be 'letting the side down', especially if the person they sponsored has successfully completed their challenge. They are also encouraged to return to the site after two months, to declare they have competed their actions – a useful extra 'nudge' or 'incentive' to remind people to complete their chosen 'DoAction'.

A survey conducted in January 2013, involving a range of the people raising sponsorship and their 'Doers', showed that 77% of the pledgers said they felt more committed to keeping their pledge because it was personal, in support of a friend or a team they were part of. On the sponsored person side, 67% said they were motivated to keep to the challenge and train harder. Sixty-one per cent of pledgers said they were thinking about doing the actions already, but this scheme gave them the nudge they needed to actually get on and do them.[24] Finally and crucially, 41% reported that they realised that doing the green thing isn't as unappealing and boring as they had previously imagined, and that 81% of the Doers were planning to keep up their actions long term.

Competitive element

There usually is a 'winner' in a gamified process, as the idea of winning appeals to a competitive spirit that is to a greater or lesser extent inherent in all of us. However, it can be quite a loosely defined term within the overall package and its terms of importance can be downplayed compared to the significance and kudos of 'taking part' and/or being part of a team. The winner can be an individual, a team, department, or whole office; indeed the 'winner' can be the entire community of players if they are all coming together to achieve an 'epic win'. It is important however, to devise a mechanism that doesn't simply reinforce existing notions of what defines the 'high achievers' in a company or community, or that could lead to a situation where the 'usual suspects' always come out on top, leading to disenchantment and disengagement in the process. It is also important to decide exactly what constitutes a 'winner' and how they are selected, and how the field can be opened up again at every stage of the challenge.

A number of these techniques are certainly not new. Indeed rewards, credits and prizes for loyalty and repeat purchases are a mainstay of 'incentive' and 'loyalty' schemes the world over from AirMiles, Nectar points and the Green Shield stamps of old. And indeed, some loyalty schemes are now rebranding themselves as 'gamified processes' in order to jump on the gamification bandwagon. However, it can be argued that straightforward incentive-based and purchasing loyalty schemes are not examples of a gamified process as there is no evidence of the 'satisfying hard work', a key focus for McGonigal's definition, as discussed at the start of this chapter.

If you want to start to gamify an idea, or if you are seeking direction on some key indicators to guide you in the consideration of whether something can be considered 'gamified', here is a list of key questions to keep in mind:

- Does the application promote active intervention, engagement and effort by the people involved?

- Are there well-defined rules of engagement and boundaries?

- Are there opportunities to improve, and is there useful and timely feedback, to the 'players' involved?

- Is there a method of keeping track of how the individual players, and/or the team, are doing in comparison with other participants?

- Is there an 'end game' of sorts? Is there a winner, or winning team?

- Are people having fun?

If you can answer yes to two or more of these questions, then you can consider your endeavour to have been gamified.

CHAPTER 3

Gamification for Sustainability: Can 'Fun and Games' Really Save the Planet?

WE HAVE DISCUSSED WHERE the concept of gamification originated. We've explored the building blocks of what a 'gamified' process could contain and looked at a number of examples of where individual elements of it have been implemented successfully in the sustainability space.

We move on in this chapter to debate what potential gamification might have to re-invigorate the rather moribund debate in the environmental and sustainability sector about how to motivate, inspire and change habits and behaviours in mainstream society. Can it help us reach recalcitrant work colleagues, or the hard-to-reach sectors of society, who have been put off or alienated from more environmentally friendly lifestyle choices by the tone and nature of the messages being broadcast?

This chapter will explore this, the fundamental question of the book: whether 'fun and games' can really help save the planet. Or is the entire theory just mere 'bagatelle'?

Various methods of behaviour change intervention have so far had limited success in motivating wider society into taking positive environmental actions. In the face of constant bombardment of messages regarding ice caps melting, sea levels rising, polar bears drowning, exceptional droughts, one hundred-year storm occurrences becoming more frequent, resource depletion and habitat destruction, it is surprising that still a majority of the population do nothing more in this area than put the recycling out once a week and buy fair trade bananas from their local supermarket.

As we discussed in Chapter 1, one of the theories for why people refuse to change their lifestyles and habits in the face of mounting evidence of harm is that, in the case of climate change in particular, the issue is too disparate, difficult to pinpoint and, despite the efforts of hundreds of the world's best climate scientists, still considered uncertain as to the causes. In addition, the potential effects of a warming world are still too distant in both space and time to galvanise immediate action by individuals. If this is the case, and there is little in the short term that can be done about these opinions and attitudes, then there has to be another route to persuade people to change the way they live to become less resource-intensive and carbon-footprint-heavy.

Enter gamification. Although gamification is still a new concept, it has been adopted by some forward thinkers in the sustainability space and tested through a range of applications. To date, as the previous case studies in Chapter 2 has highlighted, these have tended to concentrate on the home and the individual, for example, educating people to use less energy, recycle more, drive more efficiently and even to not throw rubbish and inappropriate objects down the toilet.[25] However, there is much opportunity to further develop gamified processes, products and ways of working that will benefit employees, the business and its bottom line more generally, and this is what we explore in the remainder of the book with the existing pioneers in this sector.

HOW GAMIFICATION CAN HELP YOUR BUSINESS ENGAGE IN SUSTAINABILITY

We now live in an era where embracing sustainability commercially is now accepted as a viable, cost-effective route to opening up new markets and customers, to gaining stakeholder trust, and it has become one of the core pillars for non-financial metrics reporting in the corporate world. However, in recent times discussions have focused on the challenge of maintaining such a sustainability vision to transform, for the long term, the way employees, customers and shareholders engage with the concept.

In particular, the notion of harnessing the power of the collective through ongoing, multi-levelled challenges and competition is a potentially very exciting idea for proponents and practitioners of environmental sustainability and behaviour change programmes, many of whom are craving new, engaging ways in which to reach out to a wider audience than the 'usual suspects' of green-minded individuals within an organisation, business or community.

At the community level, it could provide an alternative approach to engaging local people in activities and campaigns, people who may historically have been turned off by the overtly 'green', 'eco' or 'save the planet' messaging that green advocates and evangelists tend to enthusiastically espouse.

At the business level it provides an additional, novel way of involving staff in environmental employee engagement – taking such schemes out of the 'Green Champion'/'Environmental Rep' silo that some well-intentioned, but limited, initiatives have had a tendency to fall into over recent years. The wider appeal of a challenge or competition-based approach has the potential to enthuse a much broader spectrum of workers to take part in such schemes. It appeals to the innate, competitive instincts of humans and can potentially provide powerful motivations to kick-start programmes of long-term organisational behavioural change with multiple levels of engagement and complexity to suit all-comers. So, let's take a look at how gamification can provide a new route into encouraging people to change their habits.

We have already suggested that one reason why more people do not take up the challenge of mitigating climate change is that they feel powerless in the face of such an overwhelming problem. It can appear that individual action is ultimately ineffectual and a bit of a waste of time. 'Why bother trying to cut down on my household's electricity bill to reduce my footprint when China is building a new coal powered station every five days' is an oft-quoted excuse for apathy and inaction.

One obvious pathway out of this inaction is to show people that they are making a difference, they can make an impact; maybe not individually, but as part of a work team, community group, virtual crowd, neighbourhood, nation, whatever. This is where the power of games comes into its own.

McGonigal in her book talks about the idea of an 'engagement economy', creating a group or community, where there may have been nothing there before, to come together to achieve something concrete, whether it be a goal to reach, a challenge to overcome or a quantity of tasks to achieve. She argues the way to do this is to give the group a challenge, turn it into a competition and give regular feedback on how the individual, as well as the 'engaged group' as a whole, is doing. This is the essence of what gamification does. It can turn a relatively mundane task into an adventure. It gives people the *purpose* and the *challenge* they need to get motivated and involved; regular *feedback* gives them information and encouragement on what their *impact* is and how much *progress* they are making (and if they aren't, encouragement to help make them 'up their effort'); it shows them how they are doing in *comparison* with others and showing that there is the possibility of *success*, however huge the challenge.

As they say, 'it ain't rocket science', and we're not revealing anything you didn't instinctively know already, but it's the neat encapsulation of these elements in a gamified process that gives it its novelty and power.

So, the fundamentals of how to gamify a process can be displayed in this flow diagram:

Giving people the sense that they are not in it alone is important. That their individual effort, albeit tiny in isolation, when seen in context with the efforts of many other, like-minded souls, does actually make a significant impact is enough to dissipate the inertia and helplessness of the individual and turn them into a competitive 'eco-warrior'. This type of call to action appeals to the Explorers and the Socialisers in our groups (the Bartle player types discussed in Chapter 2). Throw a little healthy competition into the mix for the Achievers and Killers amongst us and you have a powerful engagement tool and behaviour change driver.

Yes, the challenge of mitigating climate change is still of epic proportions, and, yes, the individual's contribution to the solution is still tiny in isolation, but large, audacious challenges are taken every single day, by regular, everyday people the world over. You only have to see the rise in the popularity of marathon running, by seemingly ordinary folk who had never run for the bus before taking up the challenge, and succeeding at it, to realise that if the challenge, motivation, feedback and competition is set at the right level, anything is possible.

Hence, we postulate, it's worth giving the ideas and techniques of gamification a 'go' in the sustainability space. Basically what have we got to lose?

....

CHAPTER 4

Eco-Gamification in Business: How is it Playing Out?

NOW THAT THE FUNDAMENTALS of gamification and its mechanisms have been explained, I will make a wager with you that you will begin to see elements of gamification in play everywhere. Take the market-leading business networking site LinkedIn[26] for example.

Although LinkedIn could not be described as a gaming site (despite the fact that some users seem to approach collecting as many contacts, known to them or not, as an informal competition), it has over recent years introduced a number of gamification elements to safeguard loyalty and frequent repeat visits to the site by its members. You may have noticed the introduction of a 'progress bar' which monitors the percentage completeness of your profile. It persistently encourages you to come back and add more detail with the ultimate goal of 'scoring' 100%, an example of using feedback loops and attainment levels to keep motivation and engagement high. More recently, it has introduced the idea of peer-voted recognition badges in the form of 'endorsements' of your stated skill and experience set. It is a form of 'plus 1' point scoring and acts as a public endorsement, by the people who matter to you professionally, of your abilities, talents and reputation in your sector. This is a clever feature that has introduced a whole new level of engagement with the site by playing to people's professional pride, need for positive feedback and craving for public recognition.

Aside from LinkedIn there are more examples of gamification being embraced, and in the sustainable business sector in particular, to help engage staff, communities and others. We explore a range of them here (due to the space restrictions of this book we can only discuss a few) and have concentrated on those that have proven results. However, we provide a longer list of examples of environmentally focused games and gamification applications in the further reading section at the end of this book.

Employee engagement

An early mover in this area is the sustainability software company CloudApps.[27] CloudApps provide a full sustainability reporting software solution. No new innovation there as performance reporting software has permeated the market steadily over recent years with the advent of the CRC, but where CloudApps has snatched early mover market advantage is their new employee engagement tool SuMo (short for SUstainabilty MOmentum) in which they have merged sustainability, games mechanics, social networking and gamification in one mobile software package.

Cloudapps' SuMo product claims to be bringing an average 9% reduction in annual travel costs to their customers as well as aligning staff to the company's sustainability vision and goals in a more engaging and satisfying way. The building blocks of gamification are all present and correct. SuMo uses elements of design and mechanics including challenges, levelling up, gold badges and recognition through the use of leader boards. An illustration of the SuMo interface, which displays a dashboard-style personalised performance tracker, is reproduced in Figure 1.

FIGURE 1. Dashboard for ClouApps SuMo employee engagement software tool.

Another similar product for employee engagement has been created by the British company ecoinomy.[28] They produce a number of products, suitable for small or larger companies, which provide the platform and mechanics to engage staff in environmental actions, with the rewards of these actions going to a cause of the employees' choice.

A recent case study involves the work they undertook with the energy company SSE. The company used the product eco.system. Eco. system is implemented in larger office environments and works over the internet using social network principles. Each participating employee has their own online account and when they spot an opportunity to bring about a change in the workplace they enter the action into the system. An example would be sharing a lift with a colleague rather than using separate vehicles. The amount of money and CO_2 saved by the action is logged by the system, using pre-configured data, and the benefits apportioned to the employee.

SSE used the system to engage staff in eco-saving behaviours, with the motivation being that a proportion of the monetary savings made could be shared with the community causes that the staff had chosen.

A workshop was held to identify what the staff thought would be useful to concentrate on and that would reduce costs, waste and increase performance. Actions included: switching things off at night; reducing business travel and printing; trying out their own eco-saving ideas; and arriving at meetings on time.

Monetary values were given to the actions, and the staff involved were encouraged to form fundsaving guilds: these were self-forming teams that decided to give their rewards to a local cause.

Results were impressive. Over one quarter of all staff at the site joined in with the scheme. The trial saved £41,000 in costs and 66 tonnes of CO_2. An annualised estimate of the savings for each employee active in the scheme came to £350; this translates to a potential £7 million saved if every employee in SSE took up the challenge in the future. Over £8000 were donated to local causes and nearly 5000 actions undertaken.

Waste and recycling

Another example of community engagement tools and solutions can be found in the Borough of Bexley, London. The council partnered with the ethical eco-living company Green Rewards to trial a pilot scheme that had a goal of improving recycling rates across the borough.

The initial pilot lasted for one year and involved 2000 households across Bexley and in the summer of 2012 was extended to another 13,000 purpose-built flats in the area. The aims of the scheme were to incentivise residents to reduce the amount of rubbish they sent for disposal by reducing, re-using and recycling their waste and to tackle the problem of fly-tipping in the area. The households were recruited in geographically close 'communities' and were challenged collectively to reduce the amount of landfill waste they generated. Each participating household was given an account, provided with a membership card and key fob (see Figure 2) and could track progress both online and offline (to avoid excluding any older and/or non-internet using households). They were given points for effort and reductions in landfill waste collections, measured by reductions in total weight of the community collection, the measurements were reported quarterly and all participating households were rewarded equally if there was an improvement in their area's rates. These could be spent at the Green Rewards website[29] on environmentally friendly products. Alternatively they could donate their points to one of three self-designated local charities.

Results are impressive. In total, the trial garnered 18% participation overall, but reached 29% in the first, smaller phase. Although the scheme was created to work best online – as regular updates and other news and reporting could be 'pushed' easily to the participants – the trial found that 57% of accounts are managed online, and 43% offline. Hence the importance of considering all forms of engagement and communication, both offline as well as online, when planning a wide community participation scheme.

FIGURE 2. London Green Points Bexley membership card.

Participating households also received general updates on the scheme every quarter alongside broader hints and tips on living a more sustainable lifestyle. The membership card also extended to include incentives and discounts at a range of local independent shops and businesses to promote more local participation in the area. It is still early days in the reporting of reductions in the amount of waste to landfill through the pilot scheme, although the Council has reported the preliminary findings of reductions in residual waste amounts of around 24% when compared to the year before (September–November 2011 to September–November 2012).

The scheme has proved its popularity sufficiently enough to be rolled out to 52,000 households in the wider vicinity. In addition, the Royal Borough of Greenwich, Rother District Council and Gloucestershire County Council are currently working on plans with Local Green Points to introduce similar schemes and initiatives in 2013.

Energy use

Across the pond the ideas of using friendly competition and neighbourly rivalry have been utilised in a scheme to encourage householders to reduce their energy consumption. The US-based software company OPower has been working with utility companies in the States since 2007, using techniques such as behavioural norms and peer-to-peer comparisons to encourage people to understand their energy bills and ultimately, reduce their consumption. In five years they have grown into a company employing 250 people and are working with around 70 energy utility companies. They claim to have reached over 10 million homes across America and to have helped save a tetrawatt of energy by 2012.

OPower began its consumer-based energy efficiency behavioural programmes with a simple idea of bringing energy use, and utility bills, to life for ordinary citizens. Aided significantly in the US by the availability of accessible individual household energy consumption data to a neighbourhood level, OPower set about using a peer-to-peer comparison game mechanic to engage people in a competition of energy consumption reduction. They worked with utility companies to add metrics to bills that showed households how they compared to an average, anonymised consumption rate of their neighbourhood. But in addition to the neighbourhood comparator metric they also provided help and advice on how the householder could 'level up', to increase their ranking by using less energy. They report, on average, that they help to save householders 2% on their energy bills simply by showing them the comparison to their neighbours' bills. Translated to a UK context, and taking the average gas and electricity bill in 2012,[30] this would amount to an approximate household saving of £25, and scaled up to national level could account for a cumulative £700 million saving.

In spring 2012 they took the idea of the social interaction element of energy consumption a step further by launching a mobile app[31] in conjunction with Facebook. This allowed users to share their actual consumption data with friends and families. Taking it up a level from viewing anonymised averaged consumption figures from their local neighbourhood, here they could actually see consumption levels of their chosen peer group, and challenge them to a competition to lower it. The can also compete in challenges, earn points and badges, and participate in community groups. Wayne Lin, Opower's social product manager, noted in an article in a Deloitte review that 'our goal is to foster an environment where people talk about their energy use in ways their friends can relates to. And through that, we encourage people to find ways to save electricity.' As it is still relatively early days in the project, there are no reports on levels of take up or success metrics in terms of energy consumption reduction; however, OPower reported in August 2012 that 17 of its existing utility partners had already engaged with the application.

In the summer of 2012, OPower opened its first international office in London and has teamed up with an independent utility suppler, First Utility, to trial this gamification-led behavioural programme in the UK for the first time.[32]

Quality of life

A more systemic, holistic gamification application can be illustrated by studying the online game Mindbloom Life. Mindbloom is aimed at inspiring people to define what aspects of life are important to them, discover what motivates them and encourage them to go out and live the life they crave by rewarding them for doing good things. It takes the metaphor of the tree of life and you earn points and credits by completing positive actions, which then translate into sunlight and water that makes your tree thrive – so far, so hippy! But what MindBloom does differently is to harness the tricks of the gamifying trade to make this 'quality of life' type application an example of the gamification of life itself.

Mindbloom is a veteran of the gamification application as it was created back in 2008. The game was trialled for one year. At the close of the trial approximately 1.3 million actions were committed to, with 1.2 million of them being tagged as completed. The company launched a mobile version of its successful pc-based programme in 2011 (known as

Bloom*) and is now being rolled out to all the employees and customers of Aetna, a major health care benefits company in the US. Aetna claim to serve nearly 35 million people with information and resources to help them live healthier lives, and hence this could represent the biggest potential audience for a gamification application to date.[33]

Transportation

Moving continents to Asia now, we see an innovative programme trialled in Bangalore, the INSTANT project,[34] that was devised to address the severe and persistent issue of congestion and increased commuting times over peak rush hour periods in the city. The high-tech boom through the twenty-first century has seen the population of Bangalore almost double and the spread of the city increase threefold; however, this increase in population has not included an upgrading of the city's transport infrastructure and congestion and pollution issues have become more acute over this time period.

Infosys technologies, the company involved in the programme, was motivated into action through a double incentive of reducing both lost time and money spent on fuel. The company bussed in many of its workers each morning, and found over time that buses were spending an extra 40 minutes on the roads and the additional fuel wasted was costing the company $300 per day.

The INSTANT project, a collaboration between Stanford University researchers and Infosys, experimented with a scheme that incentivised workers with credits, depending on what time the employee swiped-in on arrival. A pre-8.30 a.m. arrival time was rewarded with a credit for the draw, and the more times this occurred, the more chance they had of winning the monthly prize draw. The gamification mechanisms involved were the idea of a reward pyramid (different rewards with different credits), time-based credit allocation, weekly draws and credit deduction. The final mechanism implies that after every draw, a number of credits are deducted from the winners; this is to allow other participants the chance to win future prizes and to encourage a steady participation.

The results of the experiment were impressive. There was a doubling of workers who arrived for work before 8 a.m., hence avoiding the worst of the rush hour congestion. The company's bus shuttle fleet could be deployed more effectively and reduce its fuel use and they found generally that commuting time decreased from 71 minutes to 54 minutes on average.[35] The scheme, whilst it was running, resulted in a net saving of 2600 person-hours per day at the Infosys factory site.

To add a cautionary end note to this case study, the researchers have found that since the end of the experiment workers start times and commuting times have started to creep up again. As the experiment was performed over a six-month period, it could be assumed that this lapsed timescale is long enough to ensure that newly formed commuting patterns would become habits that would continue beyond the existence of the monthly incentive of the prize draw. However, if the reward for involvement was simply monetary in scope, and not engaging with the more intrinsic rewards that are mooted as being so important within the gamification field, then that might explain the lack of continued participation by some commuters once the monetary reward was taken away.

In the same vein, more recently Stanford researchers teamed up with Singapore's Land Transport Authority (LTA), to launch another pilot scheme entitled Insinc. Insinc encourages participating commuters to shift their commute schedules on the Singapore rail system away from overcrowded peak times. The more commuters participate in Insinc, the more opportunities they would unlock to receive random rewards. The system gave higher value points depending on the time shift of the journey, for example, if the journey was shifted to a designated 'decongesting' time period then commuters could win extra points as compared to travelling at peak times. Insinc aims to reduce crowded trains by distributing the load, resulting in a more efficient use of Singapore's transportation resources. Insinc was launched in January 2012 to study the effects of incentives and social interaction on public transit commuting. The pilot trial ended in July 2012, with $330,000 paid out in rewards and thousands of commuters taking part in the scheme. LTA has decided to continue the Insinc study for another 18 months.

....

CHAPTER 5

Conclusion:
Are You Game?

WE HAVE NOW EXAMINED the ideas behind gamification, considered building blocks of what it contains and looked at some examples of how it is playing out in the sustainability sector in this early stage of its evolution. Now we are coming to the end game, it's time to take a look at how companies could potentially use the concept and techniques to create their own gamified projects.

How to play the game

The first step in any such initiative is to have a clearly defined brief of what you want it to achieve. The goal could be large and organisation-wide. For example, the UK government, through its 'Greening Government' project, requires all non-governmental public bodies (NGPBs) to reduce their carbon footprint by 25%, reduce waste to landfill by 25% and reduce business-related transport by 15%, all by 2015. These are big, scary figures but useful long-term goals to be aiming at. Such large, distant targets will need to be broken down into more manageable slices, but it is quite useful to have an ultimate goal in place in order to give a suitably challenging ambition for staff to engage with.

Or alternatively it could start as a challenge between individuals, teams, entire floors or offices to reduce their use of power, water, waste or paper for example, the most in a specified short timescale. Ultimately, your goal is the same, an overall reduction in resource use by the organisation as a whole over a period of time, but this is framing it as a competition from the start.

Once the ultimate goal is defined, you then have to design the mechanics of how the initiative will play out. To begin with you need a starting point, a baseline with which to record progress and award points, credits and prizes. This is the 'base level' or 'level zero' and is where all 'players' will start and progress and achievements calculated.

Then you need to define the mechanics of the 'game'. What are the rules, boundaries and terms of engagement that staff will need to voluntarily sign up to if they are to take part? Will there be winners – and are they to be individual, team or office based? How and by what metrics are they decided upon? Will there be different stages of the competition, so players can 'level up' once they have achieved certain initial goals and skills?

How will the initiative be played out? Will it be administered totally online (however, heeding the cautionary lesson about participation levels both online and offline in the Bexley Council case study on page 54 in Chapter 4)? Or is it something you will manage using offline scoring and communication tools? Or a combination of both?

If it is going to be an initiative that people engage with online, then the development of a web-based dashboard to keep score and return feedback will need to be developed or purchased. This can be quite costly and/or time-consuming and must be factored into the budget and timelines before you start. Offline-based initiatives are easier and simpler to get off the ground, but less sophisticated in their reporting and feedback mechanisms.

Once these initial questions are answered the fun can begin! The next stage is the creation of the game itself and the development of the mechanics, design elements and the gameplay of your challenge.

We will continue this discussion using a simple example to make it more real-world. We will consider creating a company-wide employee engagement project with the aim of reducing the total amount of waste and recycling thrown out by an office-based organisation over a specified period of time.

For example, we shall fix that the ultimate goal is to reduce waste that goes to landfill by 50% in a 12-month period. As landfill waste incurs a premium charge of £64 per tonne, and this is increasing by £8 each year in line with the landfill tax duty escalator, this challenge has a very readily quantifiable monetary saving target as well as the obvious wider environmental benefits.

A baseline to the total amount of waste disposed of, both landfill residual waste and any recyclate materials, should be easily obtained from the waste disposal company as companies are typically charged either by weight or volume of waste arising. A trickier job is to calculate a typical per floor, or area, amount of waste disposed of, so teams can be pitted against one another to reduce the most. This can be done by designating a typical week to monitor a baseline and recruiting a team of volunteers (usually green reps if the company already has them), or instructing the cleaning staff to measure the amount of waste collected per area at the end of each working day.

Then the challenge begins. Employees are encouraged to join teams that are physically close to where they typically sit. The total baseline for the organisation is announced and the first level challenge is announced – which team can make the biggest percentage reduction in their area's waste to landfill in a designated week, for example. Additionally, there could be an open competition for everyone to submit suggestions for the quirkiest re-use of office materials to remove them from the waste stream entirely, the winner being put to a public vote.

Ideally for the week of measuring, the waste from each area should be weighed internally – this will give a regular feedback mechanism. However, the overall reduction in waste can be gained from the waste company, who typically measure it through the number of bags they collect, rather than weight, but the figures may not be obtained that frequently and will only give the total reduction, not split by floor, or area.

A first winning team is announced, and the leader board unveiled. The next level of challenge is then revealed: the first team to cut their waste to landfill by a further 50%. And so on. Until the final challenge, a zero landfill waste week, for example. In this challenge, everyone pulls together for a short designated time period to see if it is possible to achieve – the 'epic win' in gamification parlance. The individual challenges, such as best individual idea for waste reduction and the most innovative re-use ideas, would also receive prizes.

The challenge would close with the unveiling of both the total amount of waste saved from landfill, the parallel reduction in recycled materials in general and the total money saved from landfill tax levy and reduced disposal volumes. A proportion of this saving could be then used to reward staff in some way, or be awarded to local charities or other community causes nominated by the staff who took part.

If this challenge is undertaken over a period of months, and the communication of both the monetary and environmental benefits clearly and effectively communicated alongside the achievements of the teams and the individual prize winners, then ideally the new waste-saving habits of the staff will now be seen as the new 'norm' with the company.

Levelling up in this case can mean another round of waste reducing challenges, or the competition can move on to similar tasks surrounding the use of electricity in the office, the amount of paper consumed, a 'switch off' challenge, a commuting-related task, business travel challenge or any other number of areas you might want to tackle.

These are the simplest type of gamified interactions. Once these are played out, how about increasing the stakes and looking to your supply chain, or in the case of manufacturing, how you produce your product and look to gamify improvements in production methods. Once you start thinking about what can be turned into a challenge or competition of some description, the ideas will flow.

This type of challenge has been designed to appeal to various categories of players as defined by Bartle, and described on page 30 in Chapter 2. The idea of having particular goals to achieve and targets to hit will appeal to the Achiever category. The working in teams to achieve the reduction needed and gain money for a chosen charity will be the hook for the Socialisers in the team, as well as the final challenge of getting everyone to work together to produce zero waste. The Explorers will respond to the competition of creating new and innovative ways of reducing the waste arising and re-using resources in novel ways. And finally Killers – well, if Killers join in, they will be just there to win it at all costs, but this challenge might not be competitive enough for them to be particularly engaged. Still, three out of four ain't bad.

A 10-step checklist to gamifying your business processes:

Step 1: Define your main objective(s) for this challenge

Step 2: Calculate your starting point

Step 3: Define the overall goal – helps if this is a quantified target and even more so if it has quantified monetary value

Step 4: Decide how the project will play out (is it going to be a one hit to get things moving, or are you going to introduce various levels to achieve over time, to ultimately secure the overall goal)

Step 5: Choose your gamification building blocks (from the selection in Chapter 3)

Step 6: Develop the mechanics of the programme

Step 7: Communicate the messages to staff

Step 8: Launch the challenge/competition

Step 9: Give regular and encouraging feedback, introduce leader boards, points, intermediate prizes

Step 10: Announce winner(s), and prepare to level up.

We have now come to the end of this brief tour around the brave new world of 'fun and games' for sustainability, which leaves just a few closing comments to be made. These are still early days for the whole concept of gamification, particularly in the sustainability field, and it still has to prove its staying power as a useful engagement tool. Some initiatives have already proved to be impactful in their early-reported successes, but we will need the perspective of time to tell if they have any longevity in terms of lasting attitude, belief and behaviour change however the early signs are positive.

Predictably however, given the rising amount of attention that the topic is getting, a backlash has already started within the blogosphere and beyond regarding the current implementation of gamification. Accenture,[36] in a recent report on gamification and behaviour change, describe the views of critics that argue the representation of gamification as it currently stands is too simplistic, too narrow a focus on what gamification can be and too 'narrow an ambition regarding what use of games can achieve'.

Interestingly however, the tone of this backlash, at least as described by the Accenture report, is not rubbishing the concept of gamification itself. Instead it is criticising the supposedly limited (in ambition at least) implementation of its true potential to date. This, to us at least, sounds more positive than negative. If what the critics say has substance, then we can imagine that we are currently looking at 'Level 1' in the game of gamification in its wider applications. Once we have mastered the basic tools and skills needed to gamify processes as the term is currently understood, we will have the opportunity to 'level up' to the next set of more ambitious gamifying challenges. What could be more appropriate than gamifying gamification itself?

This is the beginning of the gamification journey in the sustainability sector, and we're sure we will return to the topic in the coming months and years, when a number of the case studies and examples we have described here have come to a level of maturity, and robust evaluations and analyses of their impacts have been calculated and mulled over. For the moment, and in particular for sustainability professionals in business and not-for-profit sectors, it is recommended a close eye is kept on what happens in this field over the next 12 months or so. As we hope to have demonstrated here, a simple gamification initiative can be easily implemented in a team or within an office environment, and could be a cost-effective way of testing the water in this new and potentially productive area.

Finally, we leave the closing words to Jane McGonigal, the ultimate games mistress in this emerging sector, who ends her book with the following thought:

"The great challenge for us today, and for the remainder of the century, is to integrate games more closely into our everyday lives, and to embrace them as a platform for collaborating on our most important planetary efforts."

Bibliography and Further Reading

Accenture. 2012. Scores, badges, leader boards and beyond: Gamification and sustainable behavior change, December. Available at: http://www.accenture.com/SiteCollectionDocuments/PDF/Accenture-Gamification-Sustainable-Behavior-Change.pdf

Bartle Richard: for information on the origin of player types: http://www.mud.co.uk/richard/hcds.htm

Chatfield, T. 2011. *Fun Inc: Why Games are the 21st Century's Most Serious Business* (London: Virgin Books).

Deloitte Tech Trends. 2012. Available at: http://www.deloitte.com/view/en_US/us/Services/consulting/technology-consulting/technology-2012/index.htm

Gartner Report on Gamification. April 2011. Available at: http://www.gartner.com/it/page.jsp?id=1629214

McGonigal, J. 2011. *Reality is Broken: How Games Can Change the World* (New York: Random House).

Pew Research Center. 2012. Gamification: Experts expect 'games layers' to expand in the future, with positive and negative results, 18 May. Available here: http://www.pewinternet.org/Reports/2012/Future-of-Gamification.aspx

Radoff, J. 2011. *Game On: Energize Your Business with Social Media Games* (New York: Wiley).

Shell, J. 2008. *The Art of Game Design: A Book of Lenses* (Boca Raton, FL: CRC Press).

Zicherman, G. and Cunningham, C. 2011. *Gamification by Design: Implementing Game Mechanics in Web and Mobile Apps* (Sebastopol, CA: O'Reilly).

Websites of interest and gamification case studies in the sustainability sector

Gamification sites of interest:

Business news Oracle on Bunchball board: **http://www.gamification. co/2012/10/15/is-the-next-big-gamification-acquisition-imminent/**

Gamification Wiki: **http://gamification.org/wiki/Gamification**

Donation website: **DoNation.org.uk**

One blogger's attempt to gamify his life: **http://lifehacker.com/5975824/ gamify-your-life-a-guide-to-incentivizing-everything**

Ecoinomy, company producing online-based employee engagement tools: **http://www.ecoinomy.com/**

Environmentally focused games and websites

Ecogamer, a website that collates a number of environmentally focused games: **http://ecogamer.org/**

E.On energy company game for children for reducing energy use: **http:// games.211games.com/f/eon.swf**

Earth Echo to the rescue: **http://www.gamification.co/2012/10/16/ sgn-earth-echo-and-rescue-reef/**

Games for Change, an organisation set up to advance social good through digital games environment: **Gamesforchange.com**

Gaming for Good, a PSFK initiative that challenged the world's top creative industries to come up with concepts that addressed issues put forth by the Climate Reality Project, this presentation displays the shortlisted games: **http://www.psfk.com/publishing/gaming-for-good**

Games 4 Sustainability, a website in development, but aims to draw a number of sustainability-focused games together on one site: **https:// games4sustainability.com/**

Logicity, an online game for young people that aims to educate people on reducing their carbon footprint: **http://www.logicity.co.uk/**

London Science Museum, climate change related game Rizk: **http:// www.sciencemuseum.org.uk/rizk**

'Paying to pollute', a simulated cap and trade carbon emissions game: **http://www.nbcnews.com/id/18288820/**

Red Redemption, Fate of the World game, a strategy game that simulates real social and environmental impacts of global climate change: **http:// fateoftheworld.net/**

WWF/Allianz CEO2 game, player assumes role of CEO in one of four major industries (automotive, insurance, chemical or utility) in time period between 2010 and 2030. Aim of the game is to show how certain investments can lead to profitable growth in low-carbon economy: **http:// knowledge.allianz.com/ceo2/en_ext.html**

References

1. Fitocracy – the online social game that makes the participation in physical games and exercise more fun by sharing goals and successes at **https://www. fitocracy.com/** and MyFitnessPal at **http://www.myfitnesspal.com**

2. The Foldit Project. A crowd-sourced, point-scoring medically related challenge thrown out to non-professionals to accurately define and replicate an AIDs-related protein enzyme.

3. **Saveup.com.** Reuters report at **http://www.reuters.com/article/2012/01/13/ us-usa-gamification-idUSTRE80C19M20120113** turns looking after your personal finances into a game.

4. Chore Wars, an online 'Alternate Reality Game' (ARG) that aims to convert banal, routine chores into activities that people enjoy doing by making them into a competition with points awarded for chores completed, at **www.chorewars.com.**

5. Bunchball history at **http://www.bunchball.com/about/milestones.**

6. Gamification wiki at **http://gamification.org/wiki/Gamification.**

7. Gartner Enterprise Architecture Summit, Egham, Surrey, 2011, at **http://www. gartner.com/it/page.jsp?id=1629214.**

8. Deloittes Tech Trends, Elevate IT for digital business, 2012 report.

9. Fitocracy and MyFitnessPal. See note 1.

10. The Foldit Project – see note 2.

11. **Saveup.com** – see note 3.

12. Chore Wars – see note 4.

REFERENCES

13. Pew Research Center (2012) Gamification: Experts expect 'games layers' to expand in the future, with positive and negative results, 18 May.

14. Gamification in 2012: Market update, consumer and enterprise market trends M2 research.

15. The Common Cause: The case for working with values and frames has a good range of readings on the topic of what motivates people to action at http://valuesandframes.org/.

16. View the video here: http://www.youtube.com/watch?v=0dOfBEm5DZU. Read the ASA's ruling on the complaints made against the series of adverts here: http://www.asa.org.uk/Rulings/Adjudications/2010/3/Department-of-Energy-and-Climate-Change/TF_ADJ_48225.aspx.

17. *No Pressure* is no longer available to view but a good synopsis of the plot can be read here: http://en.wikipedia.org/wiki/No_Pressure_(film).

18. News article from the Huffington Post: http://www.huffingtonpost.com/2011/09/19/aids-protein-decoded-gamers_n_970113.html. Foldit experiment's official website and blog: http://fold.it/portal/blog.

19. The game, the Royal Game of Ur can be found here: http://www.mesopotamia.co.uk/tombs/challenge/cha_set.html.

20. http://www2.fiat.co.uk/ecodrive/#ecodrive/intro.

21. The Act on CO_2 calculator can be found here: http://carboncalculator.direct.gov.uk/index.html.

22. The Act on CO_2 methodology paper, with an explanation of the 'Compare with Other Users' tool can be found on page 50 of the following publication: http://carboncalculator.direct.gov.uk/assets/METHODOLOGY%20PAPER%20FINAL.pdf.

23. The Donation website: http://thedonation.org.uk/.

24. DoNation Survey results, February 2012.

25. Wessex Water mobile app game 'Bag It and Bin It'.

26. www.linkedin.com.

27. www.cloudapps.co.uk.

28. www.ecoinomy.com.

29. www.greenrewards.co.uk.

30. The average combined gas and electricity bill in the UK in 2012 is approximately £1276; DECC energy price update, December 2012.

31. http://blog.opower.com/2012/08/gamification-and-energy-consumption/.

32. http://www.opower.com/company/news-press/press_releases/57?web SyncID=eb788ae5-eb23-1dbe-7ba9-48a1bdd7a410&sessionGUID=20a33 228-b27e-4e09-4a06-1b9327267ecd.

33. http://newshub.aetna.com/press-release/member-and-consumer-health/ aetna-and-mindbloom-gamify-wellness-help-drive-healthy-habi.

34. Info-Sys Stanford Traffic Project: http://simula.stanford.edu/Incentive_ mechanisms/Instant.html.

35. http://simula.stanford.edu/Incentive_mechanisms/Instant_results.html.

36. Accenture (2012) Scores, badges, leader boards and beyond: Gamification and sustainable behavior change, December, at: http://www.accenture. com/SiteCollectionDocuments/PDF/Accenture-Gamification-Sustainable-Behavior-Change.pdf.

....

*For Product Safety Concerns and Information please contact
our EU representative GPSR@taylorandfrancis.com Taylor & Francis
Verlag GmbH, Kaufingerstraße 24, 80331 München, Germany*

T - #0129 - 160425 - C0 - 210/148/4 - PB - 9781909293397 - Matt Lamination